CRUISE DIARY

PASSENGER

SAILING ON BOARD THE

CABIN NUMBER

DATE OF DEPARTURE   *DATE OF RETURN*

PORT OF DEPARTURE

PORTS OF CALL

CRUISE DIARY

Jeraldine Saunders

J. P. TARCHER, INC.
Los Angeles
Distributed by Houghton Mifflin Company
Boston

J. P. Tarcher, Inc.
9110 Sunset Blvd.
Los Angeles, CA 90069

Art Direction by John Brogna
Design by Jane Moorman
Illustrated by Claudia Laub

MANUFACTURED IN THE UNITED STATES OF AMERICA

Q 10 9 8 7 6 5 4 3 2 1

First Edition

Dedicated to all my former and future passengers

"Life is a banquet—but most landlubbers are starving to death."

J.S.

CONTENTS

PREFACE:

KNOW BEFORE YOU GO

You can be anyone you want to be on a cruise. Something wonderful happens to passengers on shipboard. I've never been able to figure just what it is, but perhaps it is simply the freedom of being away from it all out at sea that helps us to lose our staid demeanor and relax totally.

You will get the most from your cruise if you refer to this book both before and during your cruise, and take it with you when you tour the various ports to record your impressions, notes, and purchases.

I have condensed information in these pages that can guarantee you a carefree and joyful vacation at sea. Having lived at sea seven days a week, eleven months each year for over eight years as a cruise director, I can offer you everything you will need to know as you prepare for and begin your cruise. This book contains information that only someone who has worked and lived on ships as a cruise director can tell you; even other experienced passengers may not remember to tell you everything. I suggest that you read through the book before you make any final plans, so that you know what to expect ahead of time and can plan accordingly. For example, you should know that disembarkation may take from two to three hours so that you won't make your return air reservations too early. Whether you are a seasoned passenger or a first-timer, you will find these helpful hints most useful in making your entire cruise more enjoyable and successful.

Later, your diary will allow you to relive the excitement of your cruise, the sights you saw, and the adventures you had.

Cruises were created for fun and relaxation, and they are filled with days and nights of enjoyment. It is my hope that this book will be an expert guide and companion.

Jeraldine Saunders
Glendale, California

Editor's Note: Travel expert Jeraldine Saunders is the creator of the hit TV series "The Love Boat."

BON VOYAGE

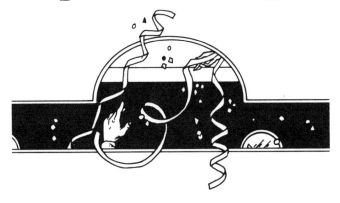

GETTING READY TO SAIL

*The world is full of beauty
And it teems with wonders.*
                    Overton

The moon is never bigger, the stars never brighter than when you see them from the sea. From the time you first decide to take a cruise, you'll find your excitement increasing as sailing day approaches.

Your spirit of adventure shifts into high gear when your travel agent hands you your ticket. Use the time before your trip to make sure all is in order. Is every piece of luggage clearly tagged, including your hand-carried bags? Check to make certain that your cabin number is correct on your ticket. Then make sure that your cabin number is on all luggage and that your name is on each piece as well. Unless both, your name and cabin number, are on each piece of luggage, you may have to spend the first night without your bags. Lock your luggage, too, because it will be brought aboard by dock workers by a separate entrance.

You'll want to be certain that your name is spelled correctly on your ticket; some ships distribute a souvenir passenger list a few days after sailing, and your name will appear as it is on your ticket.

The packet you get from your travel agent, in addition to your ticket, may also contain mail and radiogram information about how you can be contacted on board, and your cruise port agents' addresses. Radiogram messages can be accepted only while your cruise ship is sailing, because international law forbids ships to operate ship-to-shore telephone service while in port. You will have to go ashore if you want to make a telephone call while in port. While the ship is underway (sailing) you can receive and make as many calls as you like. But you'll probably find that phoning is the farthest thing from your mind when you are at sea. Matters that seemed so pressing on land take on a different (perhaps true) perspective once you are away from them and in tune with the sea.

Any mail you receive during your cruise will be placed under your cabin door. You may have been given your list of port agent addresses to give to anyone who needs to write to you. If this list is not in your cruise ticket packet, ask your travel agent for several of them to distribute as needed.

If your ship allows visitors (not all do) you will want to look in your packet, also, for visitors' boarding passes if you plan on having friends see you sail or if you are planning a bon voyage party. If you need more passes, your travel agent will get them for you. For a bon voyage party, arrangements should be made in advance if you want the ship to furnish some of the supplies. Your travel agent should mail in your request at least three weeks in advance of your sailing. However, spontaneous bon voyage parties are great; your friends can bring gaily wrapped champagne, canapés, mixed nuts, cheeses, and gifts. If your friends don't all fit into your cabin, they can overflow into one of the public lounges, where you might find live music playing to an excited group of passengers and their friends who have come to see them sail.

If you are having an exceptionally large party, you may

want to request one of the private lounges for your bon voyage festivities. You can arrange for this too through your travel agent. You can also arrange for other special occasions—such as birthdays and anniversaries—at the same time, or you may do so en route by notifying the purser's office or the maitre d'.

Allow yourself ample time to get to the pier on sailing day. Check your ticket carefully for boarding time. It is a firm rule that passengers are not allowed to board until the official embarkation time set by the cruise line. The previous passengers have just disembarked that same morning, and the crew has the herculean task of cleaning and preparing the entire ship for your cruise. The ship's stores have to be loaded as well. With all this preparation going on, you can understand why you can't go aboard earlier than the time on your ticket. Some terminals have a waiting area with a few chairs. So don't get there too early—but you don't want to be late, either.

The check-in is a perfect time to look over your fellow passengers and "people watch," for the camaraderie you will enjoy on your cruise begins here. Have your ticket, passport (if needed), and any other necessary documents all together and easily accessible in your handbag or pocket. This will smooth your way through the check-in and please the people who are processing you.

The porters who take your luggage on board are dock workers, not part of the ship's crew. It is customary but not obligatory to tip them.

After the check-in on the pier, you are at last ready to go aboard. Try not to be too overburdened with hand luggage, because you will probably be photographed as the cruise staff welcomes you aboard. The cruise director or one of the assistants will welcome you aboard and encourage you to give the photographer your best smile. A day or two later your photograph will appear along with those of your fellow passengers on the photographer's bulletin board, which is usually somewhere in one of the most frequented parts of the ship.

Now, as you move toward the lobby of the ship, you will see a line of immaculately groomed stewards waiting to escort you to your cabin. Once you have put your hand luggage in your cabin, go directly to make your table reservations with the maitre d'. You can unpack later.

Now, if you are giving a party, you'll want to find your friends. If you are on an air/sea cruise, you probably won't have friends to see you off, so you can join in the excitement with the rest of the passengers as you explore the ship. Meanwhile, porters will be scurrying about trying to deliver baggage to the proper cabins, and the alleyways will be crowded with people looking for their friends or just taking a look at the ship. Stewards will be balancing trays of canapés and ice buckets while the excitement on the ship builds to a joyous frenzy. Sailing-time excitement is a lot like New Year's Eve, only better.

"All visitors ashore, the ship is about to sail." When you hear this announcement, make sure that your friends leave the ship promptly. Sometimes a visitor, caught up in the high spirits and gaiety of the occasion, forgets to get off the ship in time. The result is an expensive and not very humorous return to shore via pilot boat. The transfer from ship to pilot boat is not easy even for those who do it frequently.

When you hear the "all visitors ashore" announcement, it's time to join your fellow passengers on deck. Go to the side nearest the dock, where you may find yourself throwing serpentine to the visitors on the dock as they in turn merrily toss their streamers back at you, until the ship appears to be attached to the dock by a giant multicolored web. Everyone is waving, whether they know anyone on the other side or not. The photographer will be busily snapping pictures of everyone for tomorrow's Rogue's Gallery (you can ask him to take a picture of you any time). There may be an orchestra on deck or on the dock playing "Anchors Aweigh" while everyone sings along. The excitement reaches its peak just as the long, loud blast of the ship's whistle signals that the ship's mooring lines have been released. The pressures of your life on shore are behind you; the magic of the sea is starting to emerge, and you are free to make the days to come the most enjoyable of a lifetime.

GETTING YOUR SEA LEGS

ACTIVITIES, ENTERTAINMENT, AND LIFE ON BOARD

A little nonsense now and then
Is relished by the wisest men.
                    Anonymous

Now is the time! Safely aboard your cruise ship, you can experience the best of life. There is no better time to enjoy yourself, whether you are nine or ninety. Cruising recreates the tradition of service from a bygone era, but with modern conveniences, every imaginable kind of activity, and room to escape for some peace and quiet. Imagine being able to travel comfortably, visit exotic ports, and be entertained while seeing the world without ever having to pack or unpack. The variety of activities, the delicious food, and the service will spoil you completely.

The cruise staff is usually made up of the cruise director, the assistant cruise director, the hostess, and the dance team, with perhaps a sports director, and a junior hostess who works with the children and teenagers. The staff may be larger or smaller, depending on the size of the ship, and you will get to know them well because they supervise all passenger activities and entertainment on board. They work hard and will give you every opportunity to enjoy yourself.

A full schedule of enjoyable activities is planned for every day and night of your cruise. The daily bulletin, which will be slipped under your door at night, will announce all of these. You should keep a copy with you during the day as your program of events. You are free to take part in any or all of them, if you wish, or you may just want to relax and be a spectator. This is the time to unwind in any way you choose.

Your choices will include first-run movies, game rooms, lounges for socializing or entertainment, even gambling casinos (depending on the ship). The lounges provide dancing to live bands playing everything from the oldies-but-goodies to the latest disco music, so you can choose the lounge to suit your mood. There are libraries and reading and writing rooms, children's playrooms, and deck sports.

Recreational facilities are also available. Generally they include a gymnasium, a sauna, and swimming pools. Some ships feature tennis courts, racquetball courts, and perhaps a golf pro.

But athlete or not, there is something for everyone. You can attend lectures by experts on everything from the stock market to bridge. There are dance classes, skeet shooting, a beauty parlor, health facilities, and shopping on the bounding main. I have found, during my many years of living on cruise ships and being an avid shopper myself, that some of the best buys are right on board in the ship's boutique. This shop is a duty-free center that usually offers a wide variety of gifts, souvenirs, clothing, and other fine merchandise from all over the world. The buyers are sometimes able to get their supplies for less than the wholesale price found ashore, so you might want to check their prices before going into port. The buyers for the shop can gather a dazzling profusion of treasures from all over the globe, all exempt from import tariffs.

The boutiques will be closed while in port, because they are duty free; this is an international customs regulation. At sea, they will be open daily, and you will find that they also stock film, toilet articles, perfumes, and other items you may need. Part of the fun of shopping in port is searching for treasures that more experienced eyes have overlooked. You may find interesting and unusual local specialties and original art—paintings, sculpture, carvings, and hand embroidered fabrics, for example.

Corporations, clubs, church groups, and various other organizations often hold meetings, seminars, or conventions on board and may reserve a public room for their private use during the times of their functions.

The cruise director's lectures will tell you what to look for in each port. The director is always an experienced master of ceremonies, often with a show business background. The ship's hostess and other cruise staff members are also chosen to make their moments in the spotlight count.

Your entertainment may be geared to give you a cultural taste of the ports of call. On a Mexican cruise, for example, you will probably have dancers from the spectacular Ballet Folclorico of Mexico City and mariachi bands from all over the land of *mucho gusto*. In the Caribbean, ruffle-shirted Calypso singers and agile limbo dancers slither under poles placed lower and lower. Then the passengers join in and dance in a circle, taking turns going under—any way they want. This is usually the night on which the last of the inhibitions escape overboard.

In the South Seas, dancers from each island will perform their own island's particular dance.

Cruising is one of the best ways to meet people if you are traveling alone; no escort is needed for any of the activities because everyone attends together. The cruise director and staff will arrange a get-together cocktail party early in the cruise for all those who are traveling unattached; this, like all other activities, will be announced in the daily bulletin. You will probably want to attend this party if you are traveling alone because it is about the only way to know who else is single. As a cruise director I sometimes grouped the unattached passengers according to their astrological signs, which was fun for everyone and proved to be a good mixer.

There may be a passenger talent show, if your cruise is long enough. It is surprising what fun you can have doing your own act—or getting a group together for a skit or song-and-dance routine. By this time, everyone knows everyone else so the show is spirited and uninhibited.

On a longer cruise, there will be shipboard games at night. There may be a champagne night, when the hardworking dance instructors proudly trot out their protégés and the winners get bottles of gaily wrapped champagne. Quite often every member of the dance class emerges a winner. If you are cruising in the South Seas, every passenger can turn native on Island Night, and the ship will be bright with leis and lava lavas (the cloth skirts men wear in the islands).

If you want to participate in the costume ball, it doesn't mean that you have to bring a costume with you. You can go to the rummage table set up by the cruise staff on the day of the ball, where you may find crepe paper, funny hats, artificial flowers, pins, string, tape, etc. The staff will help you if you need help to create a spur of the moment costume. Or you could get a group together, think up a theme, and enter as a team. If you decide that you're out to win the "Most Beautiful" category then bring the most fabulous costume you have or can find. The costumes that go over the best, and so are usually winners, are those *obviously* made on board. With the bits and pieces provided by the cruise staff on the afternoon of the costume night, you can be very creative and have loads of fun.

Every ship is different, so these activities will vary from cruise to cruise, but you can have a great time on all of them—it's all up to you, just choose the appropriate attitude.

ALL DECKED OUT

DRESSING FOR SHIP AND SHORE

The main thing to remember when you pack for your cruise is to take comfortable and easy-care clothing. Strict dress codes sank with the Titanic. If you are sailing from a port near home and will be driving to your ship, the amount of luggage you can take aboard is almost unlimited. For an air/sea cruise, ask your travel agent how much luggage your airline allows and pack accordingly.

In either case, avoid bringing clothes that are too bulky, because they must fit into your cabin closet. There may be extra hooks on the bulkheads in your cabin, but their capacity is limited.

You can save space if you wear the same clothes to board your cruise ship as you wear the day you disembark. Passengers don't change for dinner on sailing night, so you can wear your boarding clothes to dinner the first night and then again to breakfast on the day you leave the ship.

If your cruise goes to both cold and warm climates, simplify cold weather clothing by bringing items that "mix and match"—various sweaters, shirts, pants, etc. Your travel coat should be both warm and waterproof. You won't need a raincoat in the tropics; an umbrella will do.

In places like Alaska I usually wear a parka, but many passengers wear their double duty raincoats or windbreakers and seem quite warm enough. Although in some cold weather foreign ports you will dress as you would in a city like New York, ports in Alaska and similar places are very casual and you'll wear boots and sport clothes ashore.

Bring comfortable walking shoes no matter where you are going. Don't try to save space on shoes; you should even bring an extra pair or two. I suggest this not only because your feet need to be comfortable for touring or dancing, but because you may want to change your shoes often, especially if they get wet and muddy. In Mexico and Fiji, incidentally, you can find attractive sandals that wear well and are very good bargains.

Keep in mind when you pack that you will probably want to buy clothes and other things in the ship's boutique and in the ports of call. Pack lightly, except for shoes, and bring along an extra piece or two of luggage for the clothes and other purchases you may make.

If all your ports are to be in the tropics—the Caribbean, South Pacific, Mexican Riviera—you'll be able to avoid overweight on your flight by wearing your bulkiest outfit to embark and disembark, and all your other clothes will be lightweight. Bring along a shawl, jacket, or sweater in a neutral color for these cruises to have on board should the air conditioning become too cool.

Drip-dry clothes work well in tropical climates because of the humidity. You can rinse them out and hang them in your cabin shower to dry. Crinkly cottons work especially well. There is laundry service that you may want to use for longer cruises.

The cruise director has planned which nights will be formal, and the news bulletin will keep you informed of the evening's dress. The one dress "rule" on all ships is that you don't walk to or from your cabin or enter the public rooms or dining rooms in a bathing suit unless it is covered. For jaunts between cabin and pool you may want to wear a beach robe that can double as a bathrobe, but any nice cover-up will be fine. Always wear shoes or slippers of some kind to protect your feet from bits of glass, etc., that might be on the deck.

A three-day cruise is the only cruise on which you will want to "dress" on sailing night and the last night out. On longer cruises passengers wear their embarkation and disembarkation clothes on those nights. You can expect approximately three formal nights on a ten- to fourteen-day cruise, and two formal nights on a three- to seven-day cruise. On a world cruise, formal nights can be expected about once a week. On longer cruises there will be other nights to "dress up." Many passengers enjoy cruise ships because they are one of the last places where glamorous dressing is very much in style. There are a very few ships that dress formal every night.

Gentlemen are expected to wear a jacket and tie in the dining room at night, except when the cruise director's daily bulletin designates that it will be a casual night. Check your daily bulletin for suggestions for that evening's dress.

Two important events, "Captain's Welcome Aboard Night" and "Captain's Farewell Night," always require formal attire no matter what the length of your cruise. Don't let the word formal bring to mind what it used to mean. Men who don't want to bring a tuxedo or dinner jacket will be properly attired in just a suit and tie. Only about half of the men usually wear a dinner jacket or tuxedo, and the other half wear suits. On formal nights, women can wear either long dresses or short cocktail dresses. Both are appropriate.

Wear the outfit you like best for the Captain's Welcome Aboard Night, because that's when most ships photograph you as you are introduced to the Captain. Knowing this will help you be prepared for the camera when you shake the Captain's hand.

Incidentally, women will probably want to make beauty parlor appointments early in the cruise for the Captain's Farewell Dinner. All passengers want to look their best for this gala evening.

Let yourself go on formal evenings. You can be as debonair, sophisticated, mysterious, or romantic as you like. It can be pretend time, or it can be the real you. But dress however you've always wanted to, because nighttime on shipboard is your chance to get "all decked out."

Other than the formal nights, dress will be casual or informal most of the time. For example, for dinner at sea when the ship is not in port (and it is not a formal night), you will dress informally. For men this means a suit or sport jacket and slacks with tie or ascot. Women will want to wear the type of dress you would wear to a nice restaurant at home, or the kind of outfit you might wear if you were giving an informal dinner party in your home. Informal dress allows a wide range of choices, as long as it avoids extremes like a ballgown or blue jeans.

For dining aboard in port in general, you are encouraged to dress casually. Casual dress for men means sport shirt and slacks or sports outfit (no tie). If you're on a ship that has been or is going to Mexico, you may want to buy on board the comfortable and practical *guayabera*. These shirts are worn outside the trousers and are a "must have" for South America, the Caribbean, and Mexico—anywhere it is warm. They are also a very acceptable substitute for the sport jacket and shirt. The four pockets were originally used for stashing guavas, hence the name. They come in cotton or drip-dry fabrics in various colors, and they are well tailored and inexpensive.

The handsome *barong*, the traditional shirt of the Philippines, is also very suitable for dining on board when the ship is in port. This beautifully embroidered shirt is similar to the *guayabera*, and either may be worn with aplomb to the fanciest restaurant for going ashore in the tropics. The *barong* also comes in all colors, but seems most beautiful in shades of beige or white. The *aloha* shirt from Hawaii is also fine for the tropics and quite comfortable to wear. When you're dining on board while the ship is in port in colder climes, a sport shirt or sweater with slacks or jeans will be fine.

Women dining aboard ship on "In Port" nights can wear sweaters and skirts, casual dresses, even blue jeans; for the warmer climates, short or long sundresses are great for comfort and showing off your suntan. Part of the fun of cruising is wearing clothes from the ports you are visiting. You'll be able to buy them in the shop on board ship or while you're shopping on shore. Caftans, which make great dining room attire, can be bought at home, in many ports, and usually in the ship's boutique.

During the day on board ship, almost anything goes. Passengers can wear slacks, shirts, sweaters, bathing suits (with cover-ups), skirts or sundresses, and shorts. You may want to wear scarves on the breezy decks and sun hats in port (big selection of these in the boutique and in tropical ports). Wear comfortable walking shoes in the cold climates and open sandals in the warmer ones.

Incidentally, no one will want to wear socks with shoes or sandals in Mexico, the Caribbean, the South Pacific, etc. It is said, in fact, that the only times the men in these places wear a suit is twice in their lives—when they get married and when they get buried. So, while you're in these warm ports, leave your stockings in your dresser drawer. Keep them for the flight home.

RULES OF THE GAME

DINING AND TIPPING ON SHIPBOARD

> *It is something to be able to paint a particular picture, or to carve a statue, and so to make a few objects beautiful, but it is far more glorious to carve and paint the very atmosphere and medium through which we look—to affect the quality of the day—that is the highest of arts.*
>
> *Henry David Thoreau*

Life on shipboard is casual and friendly, and there are no particular rules to follow, but a few tips about dining and tipping will be helpful.

Cruise ships encourage an easy familiarity among passengers and crew. No formal introductions are necessary aboard ship; the atmosphere is more like an informal party at which everyone introduces themselves. So you will have no trouble getting to know other passengers. However, there are a few things to remember about shipboard behavior that you will need to know.

MEALS AND DINING

Dining on shipboard is not unlike dining in a nice restaurant at home; if you keep this in mind and follow the same rules, you will have a successful and pleasurable dining experience on your cruise.

Some ships have two dining sittings for each meal, others just one. If there are two sittings, breakfast is usually at 7:45 and 9:30 A.M., lunch at noon and 1:30, and dinner at 6:30 and 8:00 P.M. Families traveling with children should be sure to request the first sitting, as should those who tend to get hungry early. The second sitting is popular with passengers who want plenty of time to dress for the evening and to attend cocktail parties before dining. The activities and live entertainment after dinner will be repeated for each sitting.

Open sitting means that you can sit wherever and whenever you please (during stated dining hours). Open sittings are usually held for the sailing night's informal buffet, or when you are in port. Some ships also have open sitting for breakfast. It's a good way to meet other passengers.

Other than these three regular meals, food is served literally all day long—before, after, and in between. Early Bird Coffee, sometimes with sweet rolls, is served in one of the public rooms or on deck at about 6:30 A.M. This service attracts passengers who have never gone to bed, insomniacs, early risers, joggers, dawn watchers, and navigation enthusiasts. For the midmorning snack, or "elevenses," around 10:00 or 11:00 A.M., the deck stewards pass around bouillon, tomato juice, and sometimes fruit juice for those who missed breakfast or who want something to hold them over until their scheduled lunch.

Some ships have Lido Cafés, which serve complete breakfasts and lunches, giving passengers the alternative of this type of service versus their scheduled sitting in the dining room. I am speaking of fully enclosed Lidos, as opposed to outside buffets.

If the weather permits, a buffet luncheon is often served on deck or poolside for passengers who don't want to go to the dining room for the regular luncheon. This is great for the sunbathers. Also, if you are going on a day tour or to the beach while in port, a few ships offer box lunches that can be ordered a day ahead from the maitre d'.

Cruise ships have revived the lovely tradition of afternoon tea. Many ships provide soft, live music during this restful interlude, and you can even squeeze in a romantic dance or two if you like. You will have a choice of tea or coffee, assorted cakes, cookies, and tiny sandwiches. If you are a health enthusiast and do not take stimulants, you can have cambric tea, which is hot water with cream or lemon.

The midnight buffet will assure that you never go to bed hungry. This wonderful forbidden pleasure is like raiding the refrigerator at home, but what a bountiful, resplendent refrigerator! You'll be delighted to have this fabulous feast awaiting when you return from a nightclub tour ashore or from dancing in the Grand Salon to join your friends in the dining room. The buffet is always arranged beautifully with cold meats, cheeses, crackers, fresh fruit, and desserts.

On some ships this isn't the end of enticing you with pleasures for the palate. In addition to the lavish scheduled meals each evening, they may place a fruit basket in your cabin, except on sailing night and the last night out. Then, too, you can always order food from your room steward or go to the snack bar, which some ships keep open at almost all hours.

The dining room service is impeccable, like none that you will experience on land. You will be served in a fashion that you might have found in the great hotels years ago, but that has for the most part vanished. Many ships offer special, delicious adventures in ethnic dishes. The stewards will dress in special shirts to evoke the mood of the country whose cuisine is being featured. The ever watchful dining captain may notice your food preferences and whip up special dishes at your table using shining chafing dishes, perhaps a fettucini alfredo or crêpes suzette. And the dining room stewards (like the cabin stewards) pamper you shamelessly.

27

In the dining room, you can go ahead and order as soon as your steward asks you. You needn't wait for the others assigned to your table to arrive. Do try to be on time for your meals. When you hear the chimes announce that it's time to go to the dining room, your dining steward will certainly appreciate your punctual arrival. If you have to arrive late, you can forego the appetizers in order to catch up with the others.

Tell the maitre d' on the first day out (not on sailing night) if you have special diet requirements, if you prefer diet desserts, or if you are planning on-board birthday or anniversary parties, so that he can plan and prepare accordingly.

If you would like to study the ship's wine list and prices in advance, you can ask the cruise line to mail one to you. The wine steward will introduce himself to you at the start of the cruise. If you are not knowledgeable about wines, let him advise you; if you are, he will cooperate with you. And if you don't drink, just tell him so.

TIPPING

Giving tips and gratuities to shipboard personnel is an individual matter for each passenger. I cannot tell you whom or how much you should tip because there are no rules, but I can pass along some general guidelines that you may find helpful.

A few cruise lines include tips in the price of your ticket, and if so it will be advertised. Otherwise you may simply want to follow the cruising custom of tipping your room steward and the table steward in the dining room on a weekly basis. If your cruise is not long, no more than seventeen days, you can wait until the end of it to tip the staff. There are envelopes available at the purser's office for tipping, but you may want to bring your own personal envelopes. Also, you should bring cash for your tips and set it aside so you won't spend it accidentally. It is difficult for crew members to cash traveler's checks and almost impossible for them to cash a personal check. So it is far preferable to tip in cash.

You may have more than one table steward in the dining

room, in which case you can give the envelope (on the last night out) to the one who has been taking your orders, and he will share the tip with his assistant. The wine steward is customarily tipped at the end of the cruise. You will probably want to tip him 15 percent of your wine bill.

There are three people who will attend to your cabin needs: the cabin steward, his helper, and the night steward. Tip the first two, give your gratuity envelope to your cabin steward on the last night out (don't leave it on the dresser) and he will share it with his assistant. You may tip the night steward each time you need him, but usually this is very seldom.

Others who serve you in the bars and lounges, and on deck, can be tipped at time of service as you would do in a hotel on land.

Gratuities to the maitre d' and the head waiter are completely up to your discretion. They can make your dining a real pleasure and you may want to tip them as well, especially if you have requested extra or special services of them.

How much to tip, again, is up to you. Your good judgment as to the quality of the service you receive, and how much to tip accordingly, will probably stand you in good stead. If you need a rule of thumb, however, you can check with your travel agent before you leave as to what is considered the average amount to tip. You may find suggested tipping guidelines in some written form aboard ship.

Your cruise director can answer these and other important questions when he or she gives lectures. Incidentally, I highly recommend that you attend these lectures. They will provide you with useful information that will greatly enhance your enjoyment of your cruise.

One of the advantages of a cruise vacation is that you can plan ahead for these tips and expenses; there are no hidden costs. By asking your travel agent before you sail what the current suggested rate is for tipping and what the costs are for any land tours you may want to take, you will be able to plan in advance just how much money to bring. The cost of your cabin, food, entertainment, and the launches from ship to shore are all covered in the price of your ticket. Tipping, land tours, shopping, gambling, and liquor will be the only expenses not covered in the price of your ticket. And this is one time when you will really enjoy tipping, because you will have grown so fond of your crew.

STAYING IN SHIP SHAPE

HEALTH TIPS

*Joy and temperance and repose
Slam the door on the doctor's nose.*
                                    Longfellow

Cruising can be all of the above: joy, temperance, and repose. Or it can be enervating if you are seduced by all the temptations to the palate. But the sea has a therapeutic touch in any case. A cruise vacation can often heal various ailments, but in a larger sense it heals the whole person: body, mind, and spirit. The sea air and relaxing environment can do most of the work, but there are some specific tips that may help you avoid the pitfalls that some passengers encounter.

Passengers sometimes complain of swollen feet or swollen ankles. The advice for this is simple: eliminate all drinks that contain refined sugar and avoid the sugar-laden desserts, as delicious as they may be, if you are prone to this problem of swelling feet and ankles. Sweets may not bother you at home, but on shipboard these extra sweets, along with perhaps extra cups of coffee, can overburden the kidneys. You will probably find that avoiding sweets not only helps any swelling but gives you added energy as well.

To avoid "turistas" or "Montezuma's revenge" (dysentery) when ashore in a country whose water is suspect, remember to drink only bottled water and be sure to see that the bottle is opened in front of you. It may seem too obvious to mention, but bear in mind that the local ice cubes are made from the local water. If you eat in a restaurant you are not sure of, skip the raw salads and eat cooked vegetables instead. If you do find yourself with dysentery, the ship's doctor may give you Lomotil pills. They can be purchased in Mexico without a prescription, or you can ask your family doctor to give you some to pack before you leave home. Bring along yogurt tablets, too, as it is helpful to take them daily if you have dysentery, along with the Lomotil. It is even better, if you like yogurt, to eat the unsweetened kind regularly before, during, and after your cruise; it helps maintain the health of the intestinal tract by discouraging the growth of harmful bacteria. It is one of the best precautions you can take against intestinal problems on a cruise.

Passengers sometimes have problems with either insect bites or sunburn. To keep from being bitten by insects, you can take extra vitamin B complex, which seems to help. You can avoid sunburn by using a sunscreen with the largest percentage of PABA, which has been proven to be a superior sunscreen agent that is also very healthful for the skin. Also, be extremely careful about the length of time that you stay in the sun for the first few days; remember that you're getting a double dose on board because the sea reflects the sun.

Seasickness is almost never a problem on a cruise. Unless the sea is unusually rough, even extremely motion-sensitive passengers won't get seasick because of the built-in stabilizing system on modern luxury cruise ships. Other equipment on cruise ships makes it possible to accurately forecast coming weather conditions and make this information available to passengers. If the sea is due for unusual roughness, passengers will be notified, giving those subject to *mal de mer* sufficient time to take a Dramamine tablet to prevent any discomfort. If you don't take Dramamine by mouth, or it won't stay down, you can always ask the ship's doctor to give you a Dramamine suppository or shot. On those rare occasions when the sea is rough almost everyone can avoid motion sickness by keeping food in the stomach. If you hear the weather warning between meals, you can get some peanuts from the bartender or order some food from room service, or some ships have a snack shop open between meals. Do not drink liquids; dry, solid food is best. So the two most important things to remember about avoiding seasickness are the following: 1. Keep some solid food in your stomach at all times if it is stormy. 2. When the sea is rough, do not drink liquids of any kind. This includes water, soups, Coke, 7-Up, and especially coffee. By following these rules you will be able to weather a storm like an old salt.

To be sure of added vim and vigor for all your cruise activities, make an effort to eat well by ordering your food wisely from the ship's menu. This should include moderate amounts of protein, moderate amounts of fat, and moderate amounts of unrefined carbohydrates. Also, since there tends to be an abundance of rich, sweet desserts on a cruise, as I have mentioned, you may find that you feel better if you substitute fresh fruits and cheeses, for refined sugars rob the body of nutrients. Decaffeinated coffee is another suggestion. You may find these guidelines useful if you don't want to "go overboard." You might also bring along some high-potency vitamin C tablets to prevent colds and keep you well. If you think you may be drinking more alcohol than you would normally at home, then be sure to bring along extra vitamin B complex as well.

Every vessel maintains a shipboard hospital staffed by a doctor and nurse. Medication and equipment are readily available to handle most emergencies. However, the ship's hospital is not a drugstore, so bring along any medications that your doctor has prescribed for you. As with all hospitals, there is a fee for services.

With the delicious, freshly prepared foods, the exercise and dance classes, and all the activities aboard and ashore, you will undoubtedly leave your cruise ship when you disembark at your home port exuding a glow of health and happiness.

FROM THE SAILOR'S MOUTH

A COMPENDIUM OF NAUTICAL TERMS

These terms aren't really essential for the enjoyment of your cruise, but they can certainly enrich it. Who knows, you might want to become a nautical lexicographer! These terms will give you a start.

The *bow* is the most forward part of the ship. Anything in the direction of the bow in relation to where you are is *forward* of you. The *stern* is the back part of the ship. Similarly, anything in the direction of the stern from where you are is *aft* of you—behind you—and anything behind the ship is *astern* of it. The *decks* may be likened to the floors of a building, but they are not numbered; they are named or designated alphabetically. The two sides of the ship are called *port* and *starboard*. Facing the bow, the front part of the ship, the port side is to your left and the starboard side to your right. Numbered designations aboard ship, such as *cabins*, *staterooms*, and *suites*, are odd-numbered on the starboard side and even-numbered on the port side. At one time, sleeping accommodations on board ship were hammocks or bunks. Today's luxury cruise liners offer anything from bunks to king-size beds.

The *bridge* is the command center of the ship and is forbidden to passengers, except by special invitation. All orders, commands, and signals for the navigation and safe running of the ship emanate from here. The *galley*, called the kitchen on land, is also forbidden territory; this is the culinary experts' territory.

While at anchor, you will be transported to and from shore by the ship's *launches* or *tenders*. These are small craft carried aboard ship. The ship is usually *dressed* in port, meaning that all *flags*, *pennants*, and *burgees* are on display. Flags are rectangular, pennants taper to a point or swallowtail, and burgees are swallow-tailed flags.

The *captain* is the commanding officer of the ship, charged with the safety of the passengers, ship, and crew. His duties keep him so busy that contact with passengers is usually minimal.

The *beam* of the ship is its widest dimension. Don't worry about *alleyways*, for these are the corridors aboard ship and not what you stay out of on land. *Overhead* on a ship is what you call the ceiling at home. The backbone of the ship is the *keel*. The *compass* is located on the bridge. The *magnetic compass* was the first of these devices and is still carried aboard all ships, but it is the *gyrocompass* that is in standard use now because its accuracy cannot be disturbed by magnetic influences. The *chartroom* is usually just aft of the bridge, and this is where the charts (maps on land) are stored, maintained, and used; it is the navigator's workroom. A *fathom* is a nautical unit of measure, six feet, and is normally used to measure water depth. Seamen measure the water depth with a *fathometer*. The *helmsman* steers the ship. A *knot* is a measure of speed and means nautical miles per hour.

There are various kinds of *logs* on shipboard. One records the ship's speed, course, the weather, time of departure and arrival, and other matters pertaining to the ship's operation and safety. There is also an *engine room log*.

Now, if someone should ask you to *show a leg*, it is not an audition; they're telling you to hurry. *Ship shape* means neat. When the ship is traveling, it is *underway* and the *wake* is the disturbance in the water *abaft* (behind) the ship. If you are on the side of the ship facing the wind, it is the *windward* side; the other side, protected from the wind, is the *leeward* side (pronounced loo'ard). The *head* is the bathroom; don't be fooled by the handsome young man calling himself the head captain, for he is merely there to clean it. The *sick bay* is the ship's hospital. The *gangway* is the outgrowth of the old plank you walk on to get aboard or disembark from the ship. The *companionway* is the ship's interior stairway from one deck to another. On the exterior, it is called a *ladder*. When something yields under strain or load, it is *carried away*. *Bell buoys* are not the kind you find in hotels; they are floating devices anchored in place for use as navigational aids. They mark channels, shoals, and dangers to navigation. There are *can buoys, whistle buoys, light buoys,* and *nun buoys.* Oh buoy! What you call walls at home are *bulkheads* on shipboard. When someone hails you with an *avast!* they are asking you to stop. The *bilges* are the very bottom, interior part of the ship. The *davits* are used for the raising and lowering of the ship's small craft. They project over the side for this purpose and are retracted when the small craft are raised and stowed.

Davy Jones is the spirit of the sea, and *Davy Jones's locker* is the bottom of the sea. Even the best of ships have a *draft*, the depth that the ship sits in the water. *Mooring* is the act of tying the ship to the pier, dock, or *mooring buoy. Turn to* means to start work. To *warp* is to move the ship by use of *line* and *winch* instead of *tug boats* or *engines. Scuttlebutt* is a small cask aboard small craft used for storing drinking water. In the days of sail, a larger cask held the fresh water for the day and it was a gathering place where rumor and gossip were exchanged. Thus was generated the term scuttlebutt for ship's rumors and gossip. The *watch* is the cycle of duty worked by a ship's crew, usually four hours long. Besides *forward* and *reverse*, the up and down motion of the ship's bow and stern is called *pitching*.

The side-to-side motion of the bow is called *yawing*. The tipping motion from side to side is called *rolling*. Your luxury cruise liner has been so constructed that all these motions are minimized because of the built-in *stabilizers*. Anything that is between you and the outside of the ship (the *skin*) is *outboard* to you. If it is between you and the ship's centerline, it is *inboard* of you. An *old salt*, or *sea dog*, is someone who has been at sea for many years and is knowledgeable in its ways. A *landlubber* is someone who is not. A *hold* is the space below the decks for carrying cargo and supplies. A *fairway* is the navigable part of a bay, harbor, river, or waterway. When the *sun is over the yardarm*, it is time for the first alcoholic libation of the day. Taking a drink (alcoholic, of course) is referred to properly as *splicing the main brace*. To *freshen the nip* does not mean refreshing your drink, but the act of changing the position of a line so that it takes wear in another place. Because of specialized navigational skills for local conditions, a *pilot* is employed to bring a ship in or take her out of a harbor. Even during this operation, the responsibility for proper navigation remains with the captain. A *dog* is the fastening device used on *deadlights, portholes, doors,* and *hatches. Portholes* are the round windows on the side of the ship, and *deadlights* are the metal covers put over them during foul weather. The drains used to keep water from collecting on decks are called *scuppers*.

Posh, of course, means elegant or fashionable. The word was invented over a hundred years ago when the British were traveling to conquered India. Those who could afford it were given cabins on the shady port side going out to India, and on the shady starboard side coming home from India. This courtesy was rendered to avoid the heat of the sun. So from Port Out, Starboard Home, the word POSH was born.

This brief encounter with sea language should be sufficient to take you out of the landlubber category and make you sound like a real sea dog to your landbound friends.

LAND HO

PORTS OF CALL AND SHORE EXCURSIONS

The ports of call are usually the first consideration when you check through the travel brochures. The land tours, or shore excursions, available on your cruise will take you quickly and efficiently to all the most noteworthy places in or near the port, should you decide to take advantage of them. These tours are usually owned and operated by an outside company, but they are sold on shipboard for your convenience. Sometimes there are several different excursions offered in a port.

Most cruise ships are in port for only a short time, one or two days, and if it is your first visit, you'll want to see the most interesting places and attractions. This is a good reason to attend the port lecture, given the day before your ship arrives in a particular port. The port talks are fun and informative; your cruise director will provide a brief history of the port and shopping hints. You can bring this book and a pen with you when you attend the talk and take notes on what to see and do.

The shore excursions assure you of being always escorted and protected. They can include city tours, beach parties, shopping tours, nightclub tours, and special events like the fiestas in Mexico. If there is one port where you especially want to shop, check when you select your cruise to make certain that your ship will be in that port on a weekday; some stores may be closed on Sundays. You will probably be in some ports on a Sunday or perhaps a national holiday, but you will be able to tour the port no matter what day it is. Later, after you've returned to the ship for lunch or dinner, there is often time to go ashore again for a more leisurely inspection of places you liked.

At some ports you will be dockside, but at others you will be at anchor, in which case you will be taken back and forth from ship to shore by tender, sometimes called launches (the ship's lifeboats). Some of these are not enclosed, so you may want to take along a scarf or hat. You can purchase a large straw bag (or bring one from home) for your shopping treasures.

Be sure to reserve for your tour in plenty of time, since they are sometimes limited to a certain number of passengers—usually because in some ports there are a limited number of taxis or buses available. There may be problems if you try going by yourself instead of with the tour. Many passengers have had trouble when they decided to go on their own to find a driver. An unaffiliated driver may take you only to shops owned by his relatives, for example, or to places he likes personally. Even if you have an understanding about charges ahead of time, he may change his mind and charge you more than he said he would. This doesn't always happen, of course, but it can. So be aware of both the advantages and the disadvantages if you decide to tour a port on your own. But do go explore, enjoy, and make the most of your time ashore.

THE TRAVELER
RETURNS

DISEMBARKATION AND IMMIGRATION

Disembarkation day can make or break your cruise; it can go smoothly or not, depending on whether you know what to expect and act accordingly. Getting ashore at the end of your cruise is mainly a matter of cooperation and patience, and you will have no trouble if you keep a few things in mind. Why not end your cruise as smoothly and pleasantly as you began it?

The cruise director will probably give a disembarkation talk on the last day of your cruise, and it's important for everyone to attend. Each ship has its own procedure for disembarkation, and the cruise director will talk about this as well as about what to expect generally. The main thing to know ahead of time is that the whole process (disembarking, immigration, and customs) may take a couple of hours or more; most passengers, without knowing this, make plane or other reservations too close to the time that the ship returns to home port. If you have someone coming to meet you, have them come about two hours after the ship's arrival time; and allow at least four hours between the time your ship docks and your plane's scheduled departure time. Then you can make disembarking a relaxed affair.

The last night at sea before reaching home port, put your luggage outside your cabin door, making sure the identification tags are firmly attached. You will probably want to keep a small piece of hand luggage with you for your toiletries and your nightwear. The only clothing you will not pack is the travel outfit you plan to wear when you disembark.

On the morning the ship docks, in some ports, every passenger must personally go through the immigration line. No one can go for another person; if you are with your family, no one can go for other family members. Passengers who dash to the gangway to be the first off the ship are in for a long, uncomfortable wait. No one is allowed off the ship until every piece of luggage has been offloaded, and this cannot start until every passenger has gone through the immigration line in the main salon. In some ports, only non-U.S. citizens are required to go through immigration. As I have said, all of this, the immigration and unloading, can take up to two hours.

You may have enjoyed a fabulous farewell party the night before, but don't linger in bed; get up and go through that line. It goes very quickly, and then you can go to breakfast and/or go back to your cabin until you hear the announcement that passengers are allowed to disembark.

The immigration authorities do their best to speed up the process. Usually they water-taxi out to meet the ship and board, so that going through the immigration line can be accomplished before the ship docks. The sole purpose of immigration is to determine your citizenship; it has nothing to do with customs.

Keep in mind that immigration and customs regulations and procedures are not at the ship's whim; they are the rules of the particular port at which you arrive.

After you have gone through immigration and had your breakfast, you can make yourself comfortable in your cabin or in one of the public lounges. It's a good time to have your newfound friends write their addresses in the back of this book, in the address section, or you can simply read, play cards, or talk with other passengers. A few ships may perform immigration procedures on the dock upon your arrival.

CUSTOMS

The best source of customs tips and information is your cruise director's disembarkation lecture. If you want to write for the latest customs regulations prior to traveling, there is a district director of customs in some cities, or you may write directly to the Director of Customs in Washington, D.C. This way you can prepare for your trip with the latest revised copy of the regulations in hand. They are worth studying; they may help you avoid making mistakes or perhaps missing some purchases.

Certain countries, denoted as beneficiary developing countries, are under the U.S. Generalized System of Preferences (GSP). Duty-free importation of many of their products is permitted. If you want verification of the GSP status of an item, you can usually get it at the American Embassy or Consulate of that country or, even beforehand, by writing to the closest customs office for their pamphlet of complete information about countries and items covered.

If you find articles in a foreign port that are native to that country and you want to buy them, remember that you're probably getting them cheaper, even if you pay duty, than you would at home. Customs is nothing to worry about, it is simply a system of regulations. If you keep this in mind, your customs inspection upon return to the United States diminishes in its characteristic annoyance.

Your customs declaration will be slipped under your cabin door the last full day at sea. Complete it (one form per family) so you will have it ready for immigration and customs officials. You must fill out the identification portion of the declaration form. Then, if you have not made purchases in excess of the exemption allowed, you may make an oral declaration. If your purchases are in excess of the allowed exemption, you will be required to make a written declaration. All articles you acquire in foreign countries must be declared at the price paid, given in U.S. currency. The customs officials know the going prices, and they have heard even the most ingenious stories, so it is best to simply tell the truth. It can be embarrassing, inconvenient, and costly if you don't. Certain exemptions can apply in your favor, but find out what they are because they change from time to time. And, remember, you pay duty only on the amount that is in excess of your exemptions.

Keep your sales slips handy. Utilize the section prepared for you at the back of this book for recording your purchases, and you should find it helpful in making out your customs declaration. Also, pack your luggage so as to make inspection easy. Do your best to pack separately those articles that you have acquired abroad. Later, when the customs officer asks you to open your luggage, you can do so without hesitation. Have your luggage keys handy so you don't have to hunt for them.

Have the family together when you hand your customs declaration to the officials supervising the immigration line. They will use it, along with your other identification, to check your name on their immigration list. Your customs declaration will then be handed back to you so you can have it to present to the customs line later, when you pick up your luggage on the dock.

The customs line can move slowly—it may seem especially long while you're waiting—but all you can do is be patient and try to enjoy yourself. All is proceeding according to the customs regulations. You can use this opportunity to add to your new friends by getting to know the passengers in line with you. Many a friendship is born in an unlikely place.

Go forth in joy and find your treasures even if they exceed your exemption limit. Whether you find them ashore or hiding in the ship's boutique, they are likely to be among your most cherished possessions in the years to come, and the duty paid on them will be well worth it. And on disembarkation day, patience and the same spirit of goodwill that saw you through your cruise can make your exit a grand and happy one.

PURCHASES

Item	Where Bought	Price

Item	Where Bought	Price

Item	Where Bought	Price

Item	Where Bought	Price

DIARY

Date _____ At Sea _____

In Port of _____

_____

_____

_____

_____

_____

_____

_____

_____

_____

_____

_____

_____

_____

_____

_____

_____

_____

_____

_____

_____

_____

_____

_____

_____

_____

DIARY

DIARY

DIARY

DIARY

DIARY

_____
_____
_____
_____
_____
_____
_____
_____
_____
_____
_____
_____
_____
_____
_____
_____
_____
_____
_____
_____
_____
_____
_____
_____

DIARY

DIARY

DIARY

DIARY

DIARY

DIARY

DIARY

DIARY

DIARY

DIARY

DIARY

DIARY

DIARY

DIARY

DIARY

DIARY

DIARY

DIARY

DIARY

DIARY

DIARY

DIARY

DIARY

_____
_____
_____
_____
_____
_____
_____
_____
_____
_____
_____
_____
_____
_____
_____
_____
_____
_____
_____
_____
_____
_____
_____
_____
_____

DIARY

DIARY

DIARY

DIARY

_____

_____

_____

_____

_____

_____

_____

_____

_____

_____

_____

_____

_____

_____

_____

_____

_____

_____

_____

_____

_____

_____

_____

_____

_____

DIARY

_____
_____
_____
_____
_____
_____
_____
_____
_____
_____
_____
_____
_____
_____
_____
_____
_____
_____
_____
_____
_____
_____
_____
_____
_____
_____

DIARY

DIARY

PORT LECTURE NOTES

PORT LECTURE NOTES

PORT LECTURE NOTES

PORT LECTURE NOTES

PORT LECTURE NOTES

PORT LECTURE NOTES

NEW FOUND FRIENDS

NAME   PHONE

ADDRESS

COMMENTS

NAME   PHONE

ADDRESS

COMMENTS

NAME   PHONE

ADDRESS

COMMENTS

NAME   PHONE

ADDRESS

COMMENTS

NAME   PHONE

ADDRESS

COMMENTS

NAME   PHONE

ADDRESS

COMMENTS

NAME   PHONE

ADDRESS

COMMENTS

NAME PHONE

ADDRESS

COMMENTS

NAME PHONE

ADDRESS

COMMENTS

NAME PHONE

ADDRESS

COMMENTS

NAME PHONE

ADDRESS

COMMENTS

NAME PHONE

ADDRESS

COMMENTS

NAME PHONE

ADDRESS

COMMENTS

NAME PHONE

ADDRESS

COMMENTS

NAME PHONE

ADDRESS

COMMENTS

NAME PHONE

ADDRESS

COMMENTS

NOTES

NAME   PHONE

ADDRESS

COMMENTS

NAME   PHONE

ADDRESS

COMMENTS

NAME   PHONE

ADDRESS

COMMENTS

NAME   PHONE

ADDRESS

COMMENTS

NAME   PHONE

ADDRESS

COMMENTS

NAME   PHONE

ADDRESS

COMMENTS

NAME   PHONE

ADDRESS

COMMENTS

NAME   PHONE

ADDRESS

COMMENTS

NAME   PHONE

ADDRESS

COMMENTS

NAME   PHONE

ADDRESS

COMMENTS

NAME   PHONE

ADDRESS

COMMENTS

NAME   PHONE

ADDRESS

COMMENTS

NAME   PHONE

ADDRESS

COMMENTS

NAME   PHONE

ADDRESS

COMMENTS

NAME   PHONE

ADDRESS

COMMENTS

NAME   PHONE

ADDRESS

COMMENTS

NAME   PHONE

ADDRESS

COMMENTS

NAME   PHONE

ADDRESS

COMMENTS

NAME   PHONE

ADDRESS

COMMENTS

NAME   PHONE

ADDRESS

COMMENTS

NAME   PHONE

ADDRESS

COMMENTS

NAME   PHONE

ADDRESS

COMMENTS

NAME   PHONE

ADDRESS

COMMENTS

NAME   PHONE

ADDRESS

COMMENTS

NAME   PHONE

ADDRESS

COMMENTS

NAME   PHONE

ADDRESS

COMMENTS

NAME   PHONE

ADDRESS

COMMENTS

PHOTOGRAPHS

Insert edges of photograph in slots

NOTES

NOTES

PHOTOGRAPHS

Insert edges of photograph in slots

NOTES

NOTES

PHOTOGRAPHS

Insert edges of photograph in slots

NOTES

NOTES

PHOTOGRAPHS

Insert edges of photograph in slots

NOTES

NOTES

PHOTOGRAPHS

Insert edges of photograph in slots

NOTES

NOTES

PHOTOGRAPHS

Insert edges of photograph in slots

NOTES

NOTES

PHOTOGRAPHS

Insert edges of photograph in slots

NOTES

NOTES

PHOTOGRAPHS

Insert edges of photograph in slots